IMAGES OF ENGLAND

LITTLEBOROUGH

IMAGES OF ENGLAND

LITTLEBOROUGH

LITTLEBOROUGH HISTORICAL &
ARCHAEOLOGICAL SOCIETY

TEMPUS

Frontispiece: John Lee, caretaker at Holy Trinity Church for forty years between 1891 and 1931.

First published 2005

Tempus Publishing Limited
The Mill, Brimscombe Port,
Stroud, Gloucestershire, GL5 2QG
www.tempus-publishing.com

British Library Cataloguing in Publication Data.
A catalogue record for this book is available from the British Library.

ISBN 0 7524 3717 8

Typesetting and origination by Tempus Publishing Limited.
Printed in Great Britain.

Contents

Acknowledgements

This book has taken many hours of members' time to sift through the hundreds of photographs in the Society's collection and determine which would be chosen. Then came the task of annotating each photograph, writing the chapter introductions and setting the scene in the hope that you, the reader, would learn something about our past, albeit only from the photographic records which stretch back about 150 years.

The Society thanks members Peter and Clare Bone, Peter Cryer, Mark Pearson, Dilys and Graham Pearson and Jean Wright for the time that they have spent in preparing the book for publication. In addition, we acknowledge with thanks the permissions given to reproduce the following images:

Chapter 1: Four numbered images of Clough Road Farm and cattle driving on Calderbrook Road – Eileen Dodd; Workers at Whittles Bakery and Violet Carson – Harry Howard; Antioch Chapel congregation – Lynda and Janet Wass.
Chapter 3: Owlet Hall – Mavis Bowden.
Chapter 5: Aerial view of Hollingworth Lake – Simmons Aerofilms Ltd.
Chapter 7: Images of Whittle's delivery vans – Harry Howard.

Littleborough Historical & Archaeological Society

Littleborough Historical Society was born out of Littleborough Civic Trust in 1970 and this group merged three years later with Littleborough Archaeological Society, taking on its present name.

The four main founders were Alan Luke and Jack Trickett (both deceased), David Grayson, the present leader of archaeology, and Richard Evans, now a Life Member.

This group set about collecting documents, maps, photographic images, ephemera of all kinds and books that had references to Littleborough, and this has developed up to the present day and continues to grow, month by month. Much of the Society's collection is catalogued. David Grayson and Alan Luke, together with new members who joined along the way, walked the moors surrounding the town and finally produced a report showing many hundreds of prehistoric sites with evidence collected of flint being worked to make tools and weapons for the hunter-gatherers who spent their summers here in pursuit of game. This flint collection runs into many thousands of items and the investigative work, which includes searching for Roman archaeology, goes on under David's leadership.

The Society is seeking to establish a Local History Research Centre in order that the public at large, as well as the membership (which now totals some seventy in number) can research its collections and develop a more complete picture of Littleborough's history.

The Society can be contacted c/o 8 Springfield Avenue, Littleborough, Lancashire, OL15 9EB; by telephone on (01706) 377685; or via their website www.lhas.org.uk.

Introduction

Littleborough sits within a glacial valley at the entrance to the Summit Gap between Lancashire and Yorkshire. The area has been occupied since the Stone Age, when hunter-gatherers spent summers filling their larders in the area before wintering in the Vale of York. They were followed by the Romans, whose presence is known from Roman Roads and the artefacts found in the area. Celts and Anglo-Saxons introduced farming and the keeping of livestock but the area remained sparsely populated until industrialisation in the nineteenth century. The town's name may derive from the Old English, 'Litel Burh', meaning small castle or 'Little Bruck' after a stream flowing through the centre of the town.

In the eleventh century, Gamel, a Saxon, was the most powerful landowner in Recedam (Rochdale). He had property at Ton House (Town House), situated on what is now Carriage Drive, linking Littleborough centre with Todmorden Road. The ordinary people lived in palisades known as 'Worths', from which we get the district names of Blatchinworth, Butterworth, etc.

Following the invasion by William the Conqueror, the manor of Recedam (Rochdale) was given to the Earl of Poitiers and shortly afterwards it passed to the Laceys, who became Lords of Clitheroe and Pontefract, later becoming Earls of Lincoln. In 1311, on the death of the then Earl of Lincoln, it passed to the Duchy of Lancaster and remained in their possession until 2 July 1519 when Henry VIII granted the stewardship to Sir John Byron. Fishwick's *History of the Parish of Rochdale* lists six Lords Byron, the last being George Gordon Byron (1789-1824), the poet. In 1823, the manor was sold to the Dearden family of Handle Hall, Littleborough and it remains in that family's stewardship to the present day. The current Lord of the Manor lives in New Zealand.

The first church in Littleborough was built in 1471 and was a Chapel of Ease. Services of worship could be held, but ceremonies such as weddings, christenings and funerals had to be held at the Parish Church of St Chad, Rochdale. The present Littleborough Parish Church was built in 1815. In 1862, the top section of the tower was taken down and the present spire built. The clock was paid for by public subscription and presented to the town; the local authority maintains it to the present day. The chancel and new east window were added in 1889; the work was never satisfactorily completed and the 'join' between the new chancel and old church to the north elevation is an oddity.

Until the eighteenth century there were few roads other than packhorse routes such as Limersgate and Reddyshore Scoutgate, linking the area to Rossendale, Burnley, Halifax and beyond. The need for improved communications during the Industrial Revolution lead to the building of the new Todmorden Turnpike Road (A6033), which replaced the first turnpike at Calderbrook Road, which had linked Whitelees with Reddyshore Scoutgate.

The valley floor was mainly marshland, but in 1804 it was drained by the construction of the Rochdale Canal. This canal was the first to take wide boats and to cross the Pennines without a tunnel. Hollingworth Lake was built as a reservoir feeding water into the canal at its highest point at Summit Lock. This was achieved by constructing a channel at the 600ft contour line and pumping water from the lake up to the channel, it then flowed by gravity to the Summit Level. The lake became known as the 'Weighvers Seaport'; it was a popular recreational spot with steamers providing trips and ice-skating in winter. It is now a country park and still attracts over 1.5 million visitors each year.

The railway followed the canal in 1839 and to this day road, rail and canal sit side by side in the Summit Gap. The railway runs through the Summit Tunnel. It took two years and four months to construct, at a cost of £231,000 (or £25 per linear foot). A major fire, which occurred when a petrol train became derailed in late 1984, demonstrated the strength of the structure. Although temperatures in the tunnel were sufficient to melt the brickwork, the tunnel was repaired and normal service was quickly resumed.

Woollen and cotton mills appeared in increasing numbers from the early 1800s with at one time sixty mill chimneys on the skyline. The workforce in these mills came from all over England, Ireland and parts of mainland Europe. Houses were built for their workers by industrialists, such as Fothergill & Harvey (Timbercliffe), the Cleggs of Shore Mill (Ribble and Hodder Avenues) and Sir Alfred Law (High Peak). Littleborough was at the forefront of co-operation: Littleborough Co-operative Society of Industry Ltd opened its doors in 1850 and grew to such an extent that they bought land in 1868 and commissioned the building of forty-eight stone terraced houses on Bare Hill for their workforce. With the influx of workers, new schools were needed, culminating in the building of the Littleborough Central Board School. This was the last Board School ever to be built in Britain and opened in 1903.

All this building work needed stone from the many quarries but, more so, they needed bricks and brickworks sprang up across the area. The clay needed for brick production was mined alongside coal, as the two commodities sit side-by-side underground. Some of these mines were deep shafts but many were 'Breast Highs' going horizontally into the hillside in shallow tunnels.

After the Second World War, textile manufacturing went into decline and the Littleborough mills disappeared. Fothergill & Harvey, arguably the biggest employer in the town, diversified into PTFE coated fabrics, woven glass fibre and carbon fibre technology. The material for the nosecones on Concorde was produced in Littleborough.

Littleborough remains a strong and growing community with a strong sense of identity to the present day. It lost its Urban District status in 1974 as part of local government reorganisation and moved from the control of Lancashire County Council to become a part of the Metropolitan Borough of Rochdale. It now forms part of that Authority's 'Pennines Township', together with Milnrow, Newhey and Wardle.

one

People at
Work and Play

Hard work in harsh conditions was the lot of our nineteenth-century ancestors: if you didn't work you didn't get paid. Miners with their teenage thrutchers worked in 18in seams of coal, and long hours in winter months meant they often never saw the light of day. The farm workers', quarrymen's, carters' and builders' working day was subject to the vagaries of the weather. Handloom weavers sometimes worked by candlelight to make up starvation wages.

In the factory, cotton and woollen workers' lives were dictated by the speed of tireless machines; the 1833 Factory Act ruled that children from thirteen to eighteen could work a twelve-hour day, a sixty-nine-hour week. Children worked, went to school and helped on the farm. Examples from school records such as Mount Gilead School Day Book noted that attendance was rather thin during haymaking time.

Clog fights, bare-knuckle fights, ratting (catching rabbits to put food on the table) and drinking and gambling all gave a brutal aspect to leisure time. Towards the later end of the century more organised pastimes appeared. Factories and mills had their own football and cricket teams; pigeon, rabbit, canary and agricultural shows were regular events. For the more affluent, rowing, sailing, cycling, billiards and golf were available; these events were distinguished by the fact that the participants were described in local newspapers as amateur gentlemen. Ladies were not catered for. They had to wait until the start of the twentieth century before leisure pursuits were opened up to them.

Miners at Handle Hall Colliery, off Calderbrook Road, probably on 16 April 1888. Proprietors of the mine were the Dearden Family and miners were paid by the score of tubs of coal mined. Just visible in the foreground are the tracks of the tramway used for moving the mined coal. The structure in the background is noted as an aerial ropeway but we cannot see any evidence of ropes and the structure looks too rickety to support a great weight.

We've dated this photograph of haymaking at Windy Bank Farm to around 1910. Until the Industrial Revolution initiated a sudden expansion in both buildings and population, Littleborough consisted of several minor hamlets each around a substantial house. Each had their own farm, usually tenanted.

Here we see a rural scene that traffic alone would prevent today – the driving of cattle on Calderbrook Road. This photograph was taken in the nineteenth century, before the building of cottages at Newgate, the approximate location of this shot.

Above and below: Where now stand dormer bungalows on Clough Road, once stood Clough Road Farm and here we see the farm cart loaded and ready to set off, delivering milk to the locality. The cottages hidden in the trees are those of Greenhill, still standing today. Milk was sold out of brass churns, with gill, half pint and pint ladle measures. The same cart that was used to deliver milk during the week also acted as family transport at the weekend. Pictured here are Mary and Thomas Clough. We hope that the stern expression was caused through posing for a long exposure photograph and not in anticipation of the ride yet to come!

We were captivated by this photograph of a bull outside Clough Road Farm, taken in 1924. The three year old is William Clough. We are not sure who is taking who for a walk but are grateful that they stood still long enough for this photograph to be taken.

Ailse O'Fussers, whose real name was Mary Alice Hardy, was the last 'Gal' or packhorse driver. She used to drive up to twenty Gals from Whitworth to Smithy Nook, carrying lime from Burnley or Clitheroe and charcoal and coal from Shawforth. She died around 1879 and is buried in Whitworth graveyard.

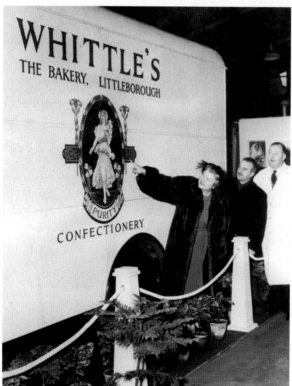

Above: This is a group of workers taking a break from duties at Whittle's Bakery, which used to stand at the bottom of Whitelees Road. Edith Armisted, Sally Clarke, Beatrice Mason and Ethel Hirst are standing, with Muriel Womack, Cameron Mason and Charles Rhodes in the foreground.

Left: Whilst attending an exhibition in Manchester to proudly celebrate the 'Purity 8' loaf, representatives of Whittle's Bakery are delighted to show off their van to Violet Carson, Auntie Violet from *Children's Hour* and, of course, Ena Sharples of *Coronation Street* fame. This van was used for delivering Marks & Spencer's products made at the bakery and had its own washbasin installed for additional driver hygiene.

Above and below: Littleborough Local Board provided the first public fire service in Littleborough and the top picture illustrates the Board's horse-drawn fire tender pictured outside Hare Hill House, whilst the house was a private residence. Littleborough Urban District Council continued the service until 1948, interrupted only by the war years when a National Fire Brigade was established. In 1948, the service was taken over by Lancashire County Council until 1974 when Greater Manchester Fire Service was formed. The second photograph was taken in 1940 outside the old fire station in Hare Hill Park. This building was closed in 1953, having become structurally unsafe.

On 17 November 1932, these workers were captured on film as they removed the last of the old tramlines, which served Littleborough and Summit from Rochdale. The Royal Exchange public house in the background identifies the location at the bottom of Whitelees Road. Amongst the workers are Joe Hardy, Donald Price and Joe Cryer.

The only identified person in this (rather battered) photograph of the station staff taken in the 1890s is the gentleman standing on the right, Joe Luke. Taken on the Rochdale platform, the background reveals the old waiting rooms, glazed canopy to the access staircase and the old signal box, all three of which are no longer in existence.

Left: James Howarth lived at Fielding Farm in Littleborough from 1852 to 1926. He was a farm bailiff for Captain and Mrs Beswicke-Royds of Pike House for over twenty years. He also farmed at Fielding on his own account and did carrying work for Littleborough Local Board.

Below left: Before the First World War many middle-class Littleborough families would have had servants. Mill-owners and other wealthier people could have had a staff of six to ten. This is Mr Thomas Grice who was butler at Pike House, home to the Beswicke-Royds, a prominent local family.

Below right: Staff at Pike House in early Summer 1918. Mrs Martin, the cook, Annie, the housemaid and Thomas Grice, the butler, holding Cullam the family dog.

Above: Joseph Whittaker was the Rates Collector and Nuisance Inspector for Littleborough UDC before the First World War. The Nuisance Inspector was the forerunner of the Sanitary Inspector, latterly the Public Health Inspector and today referred to as the Environmental Health Officer.

Above right: Tom Smith served in the Royal Artillery during the First World War and was awarded the Croix de Guerre by the French Government. This photograph was taken outside 29 Peel Street shortly after his return from the war. His house, which was near the Conservative Club, has since been demolished. Two hundred and sixty-nine of his Littleborough compatriots did not return from that war.

Right: The Revd Dr Salts was curate at Holy Trinity Church from 1872 to 1894 and then vicar from that year until his retirement in 1911. He was a strong opponent of the 1870 Education Act, which saw the separation of schools from the church. During his tenure, he oversaw the development of churches at Calderbrook, Shore and Dearnley, and Salts Drive on the approach to St Barnabas, Shore ensures that his name lives on.

Sandy Macpherson was a BBC organist quite famous for his recitals on the Wurlitzer Organ from the Tower Ballroom in Blackpool. He played the organ at Durn Baptist Church in the 1950s and here we see him sat at that same organ.

We think that this photograph was taken outside the old Holy Trinity Vicarage, which used to stand in the grounds of the church, to the rear and next to Todmorden Road. The menagerie are quite a diverse collection and we would dearly love to know more about them.

Stubley New Hall was host to a number of Belgian refugees during the early part of the First World War. They are pictured here outside the hall before being re-housed in Fothergill & Harvey's houses at Deanhead.

This is the Victoria Street Wesleyan Church Bright Hour and this group of ladies was photographed in June 1928. It's impossible to pick them all out individually, but within the group are ladies from the families Stott, Holt, Crossley, Walker, Jay, Crouch, Owen, Cockcroft, Cryer, Beresford, Greenwood, Schofield, Fielden, Ashton and Taylor.

Littleborough Parish Church Mothers' Union and Fellowship of Marriage pay a visit to Townhouse during the 1920s. At this time the Mothers' Union and other societies were well supported and played an important part in the social life of the town. People of all classes mixed together although more prominent citizens tended to take the lead. In the centre of the photograph is Mrs R.C. Harvey and on her right is the vicar, Archdeacon Gaskell.

Photographed outside the back of the Parish Church School in fancy dress are women and children of the Holy Trinity congregation; we think this was taken sometime during the First World War. Some of the ladies are dressed in the male attire of army officer, policeman, sailor, vicar and gentleman.

Pictured here are members of Littleborough Bowling Club enjoying their sport on the bowling green in Hare Hill Park. The bowling green was opened by Littleborough UDC on 8 April 1903 and is still popular today.

Knurr and Spell was described as the 'poor man's golf'. Matches were played in Ealees Valley and at the Lodge Inn, Hollingworth Lake. Here Rice Tate is pictured enjoying a game outside his beer house, Parkhill House, near the King William IV public house at Shore. The object of the game was to hit the 'spell' with the 'knurr' the greatest distance; 200 yards was not an uncommon feat.

These pigeon fanciers are, from left to right, George Garside, Harry Crabtree and Sam Garside. They are pictured here, waiting next to their loft at Clegg Hall Farm, Smithy Bridge, for their birds to return.

Billiards, said to be the sign of a misspent youth, was a popular pastime in Littleborough and billiard tables could be found in most clubs (political, or otherwise). This is a group from the Coffee House Billiards Club, which was opened in part of the Wheatsheaf Buildings, and they were photographed in the 1950s with their trophy.

The choir of Holy Trinity Church are pictured here with their new vicar, the Revd Kershaw, later to become Canon Kershaw, who was appointed in 1951 and served as vicar for twenty years. This photograph was taken in the early 1950s and shows a mixed choir. An earlier, all-male choir went on strike in 1911 in protest at the then vicar's introduction of modern hymns.

Zion Baptist Chapel still stands in Littleborough at the Whitelees Road, Calderbrook Road, Shore Road and Hare Hill Road crossroads and has recently been restored and converted into a dwelling. The choir are pictured here in the 1920s, when church attendance (including Church of England, Catholic and Nonconformist) was at its height in the town.

St Barnabas Church Choir at Shore. This photograph was taken outside the church in June 1929 on the anniversary of the Sunday school. From the dresses and veils it is possible that a Confirmation had been taking place.

This photograph of the congregation of Antioch Chapel was taken around 1910. Antioch Chapel, now demolished, opened during the first week of September 1876 and was closed in 1940. The photograph also shows Lower Abbotts and a branch of the Littleborough Co-operative Society of Industry on the right-hand side. Amongst the congregation are Eleanor Howarth, Edith Hawkwood and Edna Hawkwood.

The Church Lads' Brigade was formed in 1907 and the Institute at Ealees was opened in November 1908. This photograph was probably taken in the 1920s – note the puttees worn on the legs. The Institute, which was on Ealees Lane, was burned down in the 1980s; the remains of the foundations can be seen beside the Ealees Brook.

Players and officials of Smithy Bridge cricket team taken in 1954, the year that they were both cup and Division B winners, a fact that their trophies celebrate. Smithy Bridge Cricketers used to play on the field behind the cottage that stands at Three Lane Ends, where the mini roundabout now sits at the bottom of Milnrow Road.

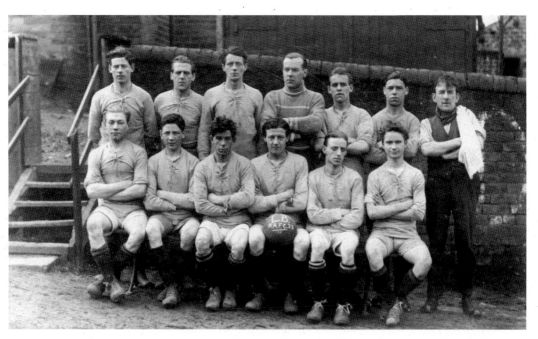

This is the 1923 Littleborough Amateur Football Club team. Unfortunately we don't have a record of their names. The 1923 Littleborough XI are pictured here with their manager and coach.

Apart from the successful men's team, Littleborough also fielded an enthusiastic and talented women's cricket team in years past. Here they are pictured in the late 1920s/early '30s outside the old pavilion at Littleborough Cricket Ground. The old pavilion burned down and was replaced by the more modern Willow Room, which stands today.

This photograph of Gale Road Boys Club was taken in 1894. They are the Gale Lads' XI cricket team, complete with scorer and umpire.

A fancy dress party for the children of Walmsley Avenue, Smithy Bridge, on the Saturday after our present Queen's Coronation in 1953. Amongst them are members of the Luke and Rawlinson families.

two

Events

In less sophisticated days, events no matter how small brought a welcome relief from the humdrum existence of village life. The ceremony of stone laying for churches, chapels and schools was always preceded by a procession led by a brass band parading through the streets to the site of the new building; ladies and girls in their finery, boys and men in their best suits.

On 3 July 1839 the first train carrying invited guests to inspect the workings of the Summit Tunnel was greeted in Littleborough by a 'large concourse' of spectators. After inspecting the tunnel a 'substantial collation' was eaten by the invited guests; this was an early event enjoyed by the villagers.

The loyalty of Littleborough folk to the royal family was displayed at jubilees and coronations by the gaily coloured flags and bunting festooning lamp posts, with shop fronts draped in the red, white and blue of the Union Jack and messages of loyalty, good will and long life. Children's street parties also celebrated the event.

Charity events, the annual cycle club parades and the May Day dressing of the horses brought large crowds to watch the processions, dancing round the May Pole and Pace Eggers attracting a good number of spectators.

One of our earliest photographs shows James Dearden, future Lord of the Manor of Rochdale, laying the foundation stone of St James' Church, Calderbrook, on his twenty-first birthday in 1861. The church was endowed by the Dearden family. James' father wanted the church to be a family chapel, but died within six months of this photograph being taken, consequently delaying construction of the church.

Above and below: The Whit Walk, in late May or early June, was a long-established 'walk of witness' by all Christian churches. As a celebration, it was a high day or holiday. Local schools and businesses would close so that all could take part. Each church would walk with its own banners and involve both the congregation and the Sunday school children. Most parades would have a musical accompaniment – usually a brass band – and it would not be unusual to see parades from different churches meeting or crossing paths. Here we see Holy Trinity parade heading along Halifax Road towards the railway arches and Durn Baptist parade heading down Halifax Road to the same spot. They would be unlikely to meet, as the Durn Baptist parade is some thirty years more recent that that of the Holy Trinity parade.

THE CYCLE PARADE
LITTLEBORO' 1905

Above, below and opposite page: Here are captured scenes from cycle parades held annually in Littleborough in the late 1800s and early 1900s. Cycle parades were the forerunners of the annual carnival parades and here are the parades from 1903, 1905 and 1911. The first is 1903 and this photograph was taken on Whitelees Road. Albion Mill, off Featherstall Road, is visible in the background. The second photograph, taken in 1905, looks across Littleborough Square towards Holy Trinity Church. The third parade, photographed in 1911, is seen on Hare Hill Road and the chimney of the old gas works can be seen rising above the shops. The final photograph is undated but was taken during the same era and shows a parade emerging from beneath the Stephenson Viaduct on Halifax Road. This also shows the shops that used to stand at the end of Ebor Street before it was widened.

The Coronation of Queen Elizabeth II in 1953 was celebrated across Littleborough by many street parties and gatherings around newly developed television sets, none more so than in Walmsley Avenue at Smithy Bridge, where the children had a fancy dress party on the following Saturday. As one of the children later recollected, it was too wet on the Tuesday of the Coronation, but had brightened up by the weekend.

Above left: Beacons have been lit on Blackstone Edge for many different reasons over the centuries. This bonfire took 75 tons of wood to construct and was lit to celebrate the Diamond Jubilee of Queen Victoria in 1899.

Above right: Daker's was a small grocers shop on Hare Hill Road noted for its quality produce. It is shown here in full decoration, helping Littleborough to celebrate the Silver Jubilee of King George V in 1935. Today the shop premises are home to a dry cleaning establishment.

A parade marks the annual Littleborough UDC's 'Chairman's Sunday'. Here in 1941, the parade is headed up by the Chairman of the UDC and the Mayor of Rochdale, together with civic dignitaries. Notice the tin hat and the gasmask carried by one of the officials, indicating the then current hostilities.

Taken at the outset of the First World War, this photograph is of the Territorial Camp in the Ealees Valley between Hollingworth Lake and Littleborough. The hamlet of Whittaker is on the hillside in the background. The camp consists of tents for the soldiers and officers and lined up in the foreground are horses and horse-drawn gun carriages.

Above and below: On 1 August 1908, Holy Trinity's Church Lads Brigade held their annual sports day on Blackstone Edge. Here we see local dignitary Mrs Beswicke-Royds of Pike House presenting prizes to the competition winners and below a photograph of the collected prize winners with their various medals and trophies.

This happy crowd are members of the local order of Rechabites, a teetotal organisation. This is a picture of one of their annual boat trips along the Rochdale Canal's 6,256-yard level 'Littleborough Long Pool' in two 14ft-wide barges. The party held its annual picnic at the other end, before returning to Littleborough Wharf.

The Children's Gala can be seen in Hare Hill Road just outside the central premises of Littleborough Co-op. The Co-op organised many events over the years for children and adults. These ranged from tea parties organised at the opening of new stores to 'Children's Night film entertainment' during the Centenary celebrations in 1950.

Above and below: The festivities of May Day stem from pre-Christian celebrations of the commencement of the spring planting of crops. Over the centuries the significance of the celebrations has been lost but the festivities continue. Tradition holds that a May Queen be crowned to reign over the festivities, which include dancing around the May Pole. Here we have examples of two celebrations, though we do wonder why the May Pole dance was taking place outside the Summit Inn on 18 July in 1908 and not 1 May. One of the interesting features of the photograph taken outside the Wheatsheaf is that it is taken from a postcard written by a young child to her brother, who was recovering in the children's hospital.

We have dated this photograph to the early 1900s but cannot be more specific. It shows a group of mainly women and children tree planting at Shore. Tree planting was later encouraged by the Beautiful Littleborough Society but for many years before its formation, Gordon Harvey had remained convinced that trees and plants killed off by the excesses of industrial pollution could be encouraged to re-grow.

This photograph of Hare Hill Park's bandstand was taken at the height of its popularity, with Littleborough Central Board School in the background. Although it fell into disuse and decay, 2005 saw the official reopening of the bandstand and the resurrection of band concerts by the Friends of Hare Hill Park, a charitable organisation dedicated to improving the town's central recreation area.

Above and below: Amateur dramatics have always been popular in the town and here are two examples of church-based amateur groups. The top photograph is a scene for the Parish Church Players' 1950s production of *Women are Like That*, starring Norma Tweddle, Anne Parker, Margaret Milne, Kathleen Hall, Amy Rigg and Audrey Luke. The second photograph captures Smithy Bridge Amateurs' production of *Ladies in Retirement*, starring Ethel Chenerey, Kathleen Kenyon, Edith Butterworth, Rosemary Williams, Kathleen Smith, Edward Chenerey, Billy Healey, David McKenzie, Joan Bostock, Ann Whitehead, Norah Dearden, Hilda Shepherd and Edith Cameron as the nun.

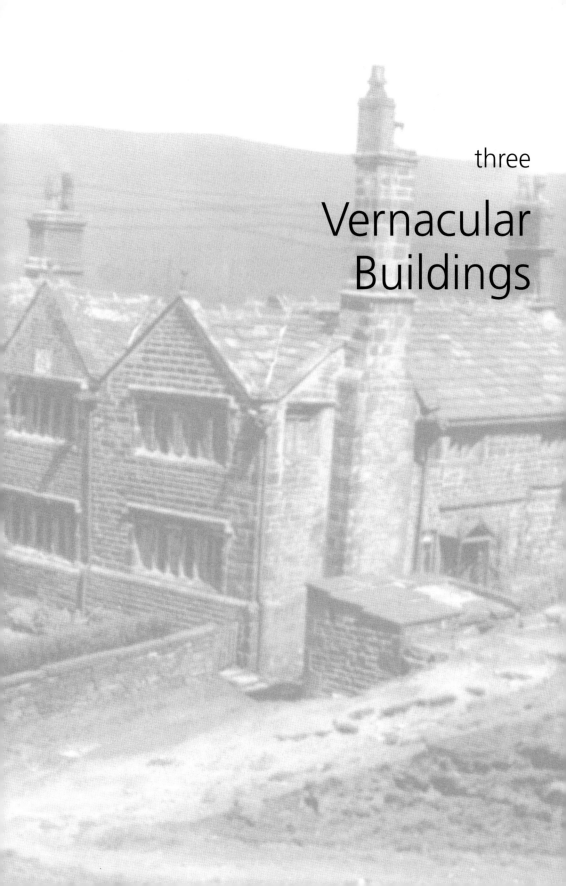

three

Vernacular
Buildings

Littleborough's historic vernacular buildings had many common constructional and architectural features: for example 18in to 24in-thick locally quarried stone external and internal walls, external walls having stone courses laid with quoins to their corners. Roofs had two or three plain-piked gables clad with small graduated split flagstone tiles and massive external chimneys to gables or side walls.

Large flagstones formed ground-floor rooms, oak beams dressed smooth by adse or plane, spanning wall to wall supporting shorter cleft oak floor joists and broad hand-sawn square-edged floorboards. Interior finishes were of lime plaster reinforced with horsehair to internal walls or riven laths to ceilings giving a smooth finish to the interior.

Many of these features, passed down from generation to generation, can still be found in nineteenth-century buildings: loomhouses at Dearnley, houses in Church Street, Calderbrook and Summit, and on existing or former farmhouses and their barns.

The townhouse pictured here is an Edwardian incarnation of a property which is recorded as being in existence in the mid-1300s. Originally home of the 'del ton' family (ton, tun or town being Anglo-Saxon for an enclosure) it passed into the hands of the Kyrkeshagh (Kershaw) family, transferring through marriage into the Newall family, and later through marriage into the Molesworth family. It was then bought by brothers Gordon and Ernst Harvey in 1902, when it was remodelled into its current appearance.

Above and below: Briercliffe House stands on Church Street and was built in the late 1860s as a private house. It was occupied by Dr Bryan Lister, who died in 1874, and at this time the house and stables were valued at £325. The house was then used by the resident preacher of the Littleborough United Methodist Church on Church Street, almost opposite the house, and then by the Scarr family of doctors. The photograph shows the separate surgery entrance, now removed. The property is now occupied by the Vine Fellowship, a Christian organisation, with the stables converted into a bookshop and tea rooms.

Lane Foot Farm is situated in the Ealees Valley. This photograph shows the farm buildings and, obscured by the haze, Hollingworth Lake. Behind the photographer is Owlet Hall.

High Lee Farm pictured in 1912. High Lee is situated on the edge of Shore Moor, between Shore Hall and Clough. Our records suggest that it was in the ownership of the Burrill family at the time the photograph was taken; ten members of the family and farm workers look happy to have their photograph taken.

New Platt Farm is a smallholding on Carriage Drive, halfway between Todmorden Road and Townhouse. The view of the farm here is taken from Townhouse Brook as it culverts Todmorden Road lower down. Gale House is visible through the trees.

Nestling at the foot of Syke Moor and behind Hollingworth Fold, this is one of several images of Syke Farm from the Society's archives. As with many photographs, today the building is obscured from view by the growth of trees and shrubbery. Quarrying is evidenced nearby and the remains of kilns point to the area's previous exploitation of natural materials.

The Queens Cinema was built in 1912 with a frontage onto Church Street and rear exit doors in James Hill Street. The cinema retained a right of way across the old farmyard of the Royal Oak by means of an emergency exit leading to either the back door of the Royal Oak or Church Street. The cinema had two performances each day, Monday to Saturday evenings, with a matinee on Saturday afternoons and a change of film on Thursday, so cinema-goers could see two films a week. After the closure of the cinema, the building became a car showroom before eventually being destroyed by fire.

Barehill Street and the cul-de-sacs running off it was set out by Littleborough Co-operative Society of Industry to provide forty-eight houses for its workers. On the opposite side is the old toffee factory in 1932 and, next to it, the cobbler's shop of Wilson Bamford. To the left-hand side is land on which the old labour exchange was erected later in the 1930s.

Prospect House was built by John Tetlow who owned and operated a brickworks on a site adjacent to the house and the Rochdale Canal. The house occupied the upper three storeys, with servants' quarters situated on a lower floor, built back-to-earth.

Durn Lea was a complex of five houses, built in an 'L' shape, with gardens whose amenities included a private tennis court. They were situated on land opposite Lea House on Todmorden Road. After the Second World War one of the houses was converted into a local office of the Inland Revenue, the remainder used as a hostel for displaced persons.

The Beach Hotel dates back to the mid-1800s and was part of the Sladen empire. James Sladen, a local businessman, played on the growing popularity of Hollingworth Lake as a tourist attraction and provided entertainment, boat rides, dancing stages and all manner of attractions to help tourists and locals alike to enjoy themselves and part with their money.

The origin of this hotel at Hollingworth Lake can be traced to the purchase of 600 square yards of land from a gentleman by the name of Hardman by a certain William Whipp in 1872. The Whipps sold the hotel in 1886 for £2,200 and it was again auctioned in 1888. The sales notice of 1888 describes the premises as 'well adapted for doing a large business, has a large and commanding frontage, is three storeys high and contains twenty-three rooms. The Lake being a popular holiday resort, the takings at Easter, which is close at hand, and other holiday seasons are very great.'

Situated at the back of the lake, the Lake Hotel, with its dancing stages and Swiss-style buildings, was developed in the heyday of Victorian popularity for the lake and its surroundings and eventually became part of the Sladen empire of local leisure facilities. In 1939 the renewal of the license was refused because of structural deficiencies; it still managed to carry on as a restaurant for a further thirty years before demolition in 1970.

The Mermaid Inn was situated on Syke Road at Hollingworth Fold, the old road out of Hollingworth to Ogden, and was probably the last place of refreshment until the Ram's Head at Denshaw. The inn closed in 1911 and the building was demolished in 1940.

The Old Blue Ball stood on Smithy Bridge Road opposite Walmsley Avenue. The earliest reference to the pub is to a Mrs Holt, a victualler of Walms Lane, in 1818. The 1851 census confirms James Collinge at the Blue Ball, Walmsley Lane; he appears to have married the previous landlord's widow. He helped his income by also keeping the trade of fulling miller.

This was one of a group of cottages that are mentioned in the 1880 rating list as: 'Daniel Spencer; Three Lane Ends; Public House; Gross Rental £30; Self Owner; Sarah Nuttall and others, occupiers; 3 houses £15 10 00'. It was situated at the junction of Smithy Bridge Road and Milnrow Road where today stands a nursing home. The pub's licence expired in December 1924 but the buildings survived into the 1950s.

Above: The Horseshoe public house stood on Featherstall Road adjacent to the Sun Hotel and was described by Rochdale dialect author Edwin Waugh as 'an old-fashioned public house, apparently as old as the present Stubley Hall'.

Left: The Blue Bell public house and old Dearnley post office were housed in a late eighteenth/early nineteenth-century three-storey loomhouse with full-width mullioned windows to the upper floor. In the mid-1860s, this floor was used by a breakaway faction of the Stubley Primitive Methodists and later as a day school and mission hall by the Revd Canon Cook of Smallbridge; the first forty pupils were taught by a Miss Emily Redfern. Along with Dearnley Co-op, these buildings were demolished in 1974 to make way for the Crowther Court flats.

Falcon Cottage was built in 1866 for John Fletcher, landlord of the Falcon Inn. Visible is the ornate date stone over one of the doors. The architect was Frank H. Shuttleworth of Littleborough. The house is now used by Kelsall's Bookshop as an annex, the interior remaining unchanged and with its original Victorian plasterwork and woodwork.

The Dyers Arms was opened by Sally Taylor, a widow, in 1825, following alterations to an inherited property after subsidence caused by the Dearnley Colliery Co., who paid £60 compensation to her for damage done. The photograph depicts a cart carrying spirit bottles and advertising Whitbread's Ales, claiming W. Taylor of the Dyers Arms as sole agent.

The Woodcock Inn was in the valley below the A58 at Sladen Fold, know locally as the 'Gap'. The area is mentioned in early records as the Watergate. After a fire, in which the lives of the Colclough family were saved by their whippet, which raised the alarm, the rebuilding discovered church wardens' pipes in a cavity in the wall.

This is the former Shepherds Rest on Blackstone Edge Road. Also known as Fence Nook or the Shepherds Tavern, it was a public house until 1915, later the Nook Restaurant and now recently converted into dwellings. This photograph was taken in the early 1900s, certainly pre-First World War; the landlady depicted lost her son in that conflict.

Windy Bank is one of the oldest houses in Littleborough and is a listed building. Records of the occupation of the site go back to 1335 when a Henry de Wyndebonks is recorded in the court rolls. In the Middle Ages it was home to the Lyghtollers family before they moved to the newly built Lightowlers, on the opposite side of Halifax Road.

Pike House stood on Blackstone Edge Road, just beyond Bent House. It was the family home of the Halliwells, and later the Beswicke-Royds, from 1596 until the family died out in 1940. In its last years it was a restaurant before a fire caused it to be demolished in the 1960s. Gateposts of the original driveway are still visible in a wall by the main road. The elevation pictured here is a façade built by John Halliwell in 1703/08 and it conceals the three-piked gable roof of the original house.

Clegg Hall was probably erected in the early 1600s by Theophilus Assheton and has had a chequered history. In 1818 it was a public house known as the Hare and Hounds and later The Black Sloven (named after a tenant's horse). Steeped in tales of mystery, it is currently a ruin undergoing restoration as a dwelling.

Owlet Hall in the late 1800s. Situated on the Whittaker estate close to Ealees, it is a farmstead known originally as Oken Holt and recorded as early as 1615 in a land transfer within the Schofield family.

Heather Mount was occupied by the owners of Heap Dyers and Finishers. It stands in the small hamlet of Whittaker, on the lower slopes of Blackstone Edge overlooking Hollingworth Lake and the Ealees Valley.

Honresfeld was built in 1870 by brothers William and Alfred Law, woollen manufacturers of Lydgate and Durn Mills. After their death, the house was inherited by William's son, Sir Alfred Law JP, MP for the High Peak constituency, who lived there until his own death; the house was then occupied by a member of the management team of Law's Durn Mill. The house was eventually transferred into the ownership of the Leonard Cheshire Foundation and is used today as a care home.

Along with Shore Mills, owned by the Clegg Family, Shore House has now been demolished and the land, off Shore Road, has been developed into further dwellings. The only reminder of the past industry is the small war memorial to those of Shore Mills who gave their lives for Britain during the First World War, which still stands close to the site of the house.

Sladen Wood House stood on Todmorden Road adjacent to Sladen Wood Mill and was part of the Fothergill & Harvey empire. It provided a home in the latter half of the nineteenth century to Jessie Fothergill, daughter of the original Fothergill and an accomplished romantic author in her own right. Though no longer in existence, the house backed onto the Rochdale Canal and visible is part of Tetlow's Brickworks on the far side of the cut.

The White House is an old coaching inn, indeed it was the Coach and Horses until December 1920, when its name was changed to reflect that by which it was always known. This photograph shows the building as it originally stood, before the central courtyard was walled in to extend the premises. Scene of many incidents, the most famous was the attempted murder of the landlady, Mrs MacIntyre, on 6 December 1894. The Annals of Rochdale record that the assailant was a Mr R. Ackrigg, who was sentenced to twelve years penal servitude on 23 February 1895.

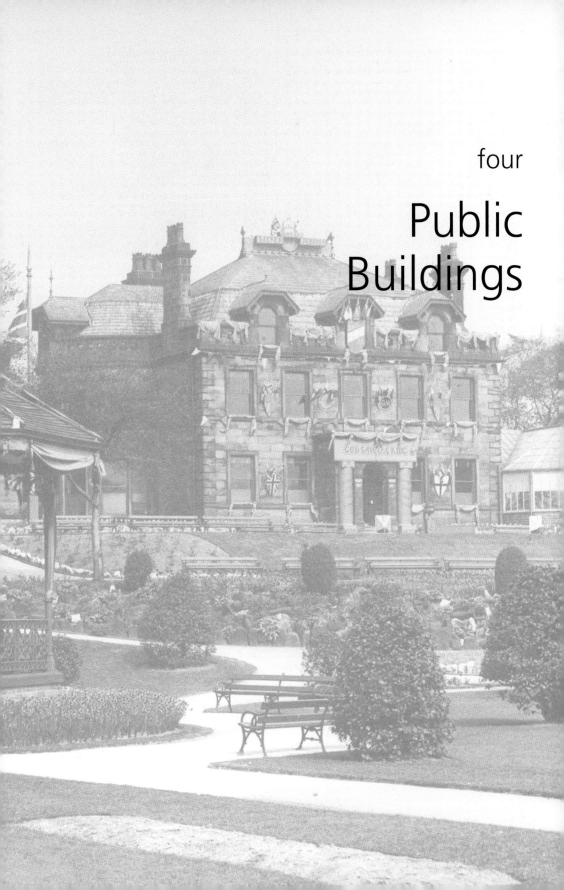

four

Public
Buildings

In the mid-eighteenth century, it was stated that Littleborough had 182 families, four dissenters, no Quakers and no Papists. From 1471 until 1808, the Church of the Holy Trinity was the only place of worship in Littleborough; in the nineteenth century a further twenty-nine places of worship were built to cater for the increasing population. The Church of England had churches at Calderbrook, Shore and Dearnley. By the mid-1870s, the Catholics had sufficient numbers to rent a room, Sundays only, in Brown Street. By 1881, they had built the first of their three churches on a plot of land at Featherstall. In the early nineteenth century, Methodist preachers from Walsden, Todmorden and Rochdale had founded missions in Calderbrook, Summit and Littleborough, and Baptist preachers from Ogden had a mission at Durn.

These chapels served their congregations until rising costs and diminishing congregations forced their closures: out of the twenty-five Nonconformist chapels built in Littleborough, only four remain serving their congregations, the others were either demolished or converted to other usage.

On the Feast of St Chad in March 1471, the Dean and Convent of Whalley granted 'to the inhabitants of the village of Butterworth and Honorsfeld within the Parish of Rochdale leave to have certain masses said in a Chapel newly built in the town of Honorsfeld'. This is a sketch of the original chapel, drawn to demonstrate its poor state of repairs when the church commissioners were being petitioned to allow construction of a new church in the early 1800s.

Opposite top and opposite left: In 1800, the Vicar of Rochdale, Dr Dunster, noted that Littleborough Chapel was 'in the most wretched of conditions … a danger to the people' and so a new church was built between 1815 and 1820, 15 yards north of the old chapel. The clock is a town clock and was paid for in 1862 by Henry Newall of Hare Hill House. The church was enlarged in 1889 with the building of a new chancel and the new East Window pictured here was paid for by the Cleggs of Shore Mills.

Opposite right: As well as the town's cenotaph, each church erected its own memorial to parishioners who fell in the First World War. Here is the Holy Trinity memorial shortly after erection in 1921. Clearly visible on the pedestal are the names of the fallen. Time and weather have now removed these names, but the memorial still stands in the graveyard on the corner of Halifax Road and Todmorden Road.

PARISH CHURCH & SQUARE
LITTLEBOROUGH

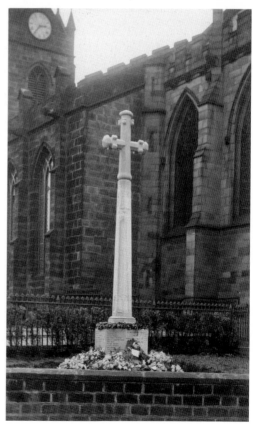

Although the Revd Carter of Holy Trinity had been preaching at Shore for thirty years, it was not until 1900 that the decision to build a church was taken. St Barnabas was consecrated in 1901 and declared a parish, with the Revd Petts in charge. The driveway to the church is now lined with private houses.

Above: St Andrew's Church at Dearnley was built in two stages on a plot of land formed by Arm Road Meadow and Lower Arm Road Field and was consecrated on 25 September 1895. The first vicar was the Revd Oakley, who was nephew to the church's architect. Revd Oakley commenced preaching in a 'tin church' at Dearnley before construction of the current church commenced.

Left: Calderbrook's St James' Church was to be the Dearden family's own chapel but the death of James Dearden shortly after the laying of the foundation stone in 1861 delayed construction. It became a Chapel of Ease to Holy Trinity in 1865, was consecrated in 1870 and became a parish church in its own right in 1896.

Above and below: A barn and stables occupied this piece of land in 1805, followed in 1809 by the 'Methodical Piazza', the chapel of the Littleborough Wesleyan Methodists. The Piazza was the first place of worship to be built in Littleborough since the original Holy Trinity Church. The chapel was entered by a door opening directly onto Canal Street, the viaduct not yet having been built, or by two doors in the wall fronting the river, approached via a footpath and wooden bridge (courtesy of Anne Lord) over the river from Church Street. This bridge was washed away during a flood and was replaced by a cast-iron and stone-flagged bridge further upstream. The Wesleyans used the Piazza as a place of worship until the noise of passing trains caused them to close in the mid-1800s. In about 1830 a shop and three cottages were also built on the plot. Doors facing Church Street gave access to the shop and one of the cottages. A cantilevered stone-flagged footpath, the remains of which can still be seen today, accessed the other two cottages with doors overlooking the river.

To overcome being overshadowed by the railway arches and to avoid the noise of passing trains, the Wesleyans undertook the building of their new chapel in Victoria Street at a cost of £1,850 in 1865; the stone-laying ceremony took place on 15 April that year. The congregation grew larger and the chapel was extended by a further 18ft in 1885 and it closed exactly a century later.

Dearnley Methodist Church on New Road after being extended from the original building on the left-hand side. The architect was Butterworth, responsible for many buildings in Littleborough including the now-demolished Bleaked Hill Isolation Hospital off Milnrow Road. The Methodist church congregation commenced worship at the Blue Bell public house before erecting a chapel.

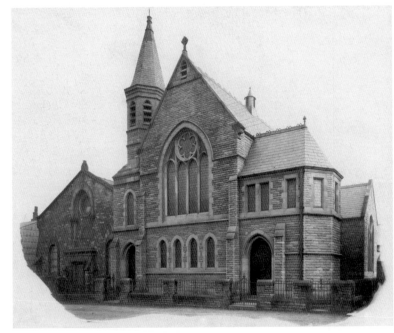

This is Summit Primitive Methodists, a 48ft x 36ft two-storey chapel, which was built in 1866 at a cost of £600. The chapel was first served by the Knowlwood Circuit of preachers, followed by the Todmorden Circuit and then from 1883, the Littleborough Circuit. The first service was held on Good Friday in 1867 and the last on Sunday 27 May 1990 and the chapel has now been converted into a private dwelling.

This is a photograph of the inside of Summit Temple Methodist Chapel. After ninety years of meeting in the farms and houses of fellow Wesleyans, the Temple Wesleyans built their Providence Temple Chapel in 1839 on Temple Lane. A second Providence chapel was built in 1871 when the original chapel became too small for the congregation. Both were sold off in 1961 and demolished to make way for private housing.

Dearnley Workhouse of the Rochdale Union opened its door to the poor of the area on 1 November 1877, replacing many older and smaller workhouses from across the borough. The older workhouses were located at Hollingworth, Stansfield, Wardle, Marland, Spotland and Wardleworth. Dearnley Workhouse originally cost around £85,000. It was increased in size in 1902 by the addition of a hospital block and again in 1931 with a children's ward and maternity home. The workhouse was amalgamated with the hospital on formation of the National Health Service in 1948.

Hollingworth Workhouse had a date stone of 1697 and opened as a workhouse in 1778. It was part of Hill's Hollingworth Estate and closed in 1874, when inmates were transferred to Marland Workhouse. Reports of the conditions within the workhouse were never good and it failed even to meet the minimal standards required by the Poor Law.

Above and below: Where now stands the Dale View housing estate on Milnrow Road once stood Bleaked Hill Isolation Hospital. Here we see the entrance gates and lodge house, together with a typical ward scene, decorated to celebrate an unknown event. The gateposts of the old hospital are still to be seen, incorporated into the wall that separates the rear gardens of Knowl View from the main road, opposite Peanock Lane. The isolation hospital later changed its name to Lakeview Hospital before closing and was demolished in the 1960s.

Above and below: Hare Hill House in the grounds of Hare Hill Park was built in the 1800s by Henry Newall, mill-owner, and was occupied by his family until the end of the nineteenth century when it was leased to Littleborough UDC for the annual sum of £323 9s 8d and remains to this day as the local offices of Rochdale MBC. The grounds of the house were set out into Hare Hill Park at the start of the twentieth century with the addition of a bandstand and a drinking fountain. The bandstand was presented to the town by James Cryer to commemorate the Coronation of King Edward VII in 1902. The fountain in Hare Hill Park was donated to Littleborough UDC at a cost of £170 and erected in 1903. It commemorated the Golden Jubilee in 1900 of Littleborough Co-operative Society of Industry.

Above and below: Hare Hill House is pictured here in 1935, decorated to celebrate the Silver Jubilee of King George V, and later during the Second World War when it was not only the offices of the UDC but also an ARP post. Banners and decorative streamers bedeck the building to celebrate the Jubilee and sandbags and window protection masks the building during the later conflict.

Left and below: The house was the first in the town to have a proper internal plumbing arrangement with water stored in roof tanks to feed sinks, toilets and baths throughout the house. Water was pumped from a passing stream by the waterwheel which still remains in the park grounds. The formal opening of the recreational grounds was held a week before the Council took possession of Hare Hill House. A grand procession from Littleborough Square to Hare Hill, led by Littleborough Prize Band, was organised, and after a few speeches the deeds of the property were handed over to the Council's chairman as representative of the trustees (for the public).

Above and below: These two photographs show the extension to Hare Hill House by Littleborough UDC to form a public library. The architects were Butterworth & Duncan of Rochdale and the official opening took place on 12 December 1903, performed by Alexander Gordon Cummins Harvey, with the date being cast into the cast-iron rainwater pipe heads. The cost of the building was £2,608, defrayed by a grant from the Andrew Carnegie Foundation. When the library was first opened, all available books were listed on an indicator. The borrower checked the indicator against a catalogue and if his/her chosen book was available gave its title to the librarian who would then find the book on the shelves and pass it over the counter to the borrower.

LITTLEBOROUGH PARK ENTRANCE

BYE-LAWS

Made by the Urban District Council of Littleborough with respect to the

Pleasure Ground

AT HARE HILL.

Above and left: These are photographs of the entrance to Hare Hill Park, off Hare Hill Road, and a copy of the bye-laws passed by Littleborough UDC to regulate use and enjoyment of Hare Hill Park, known then as a pleasure ground. The rules were posted by the park entrance and can be seen on the left-hand side of the gateposts.

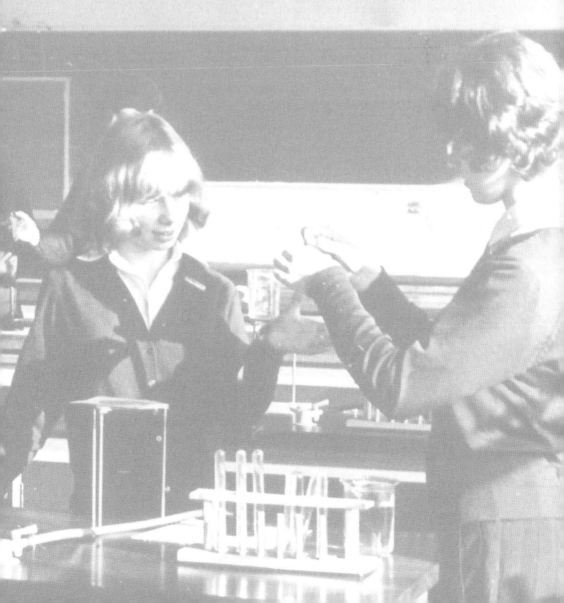

five

Schools

Halliwell's Endowed School opened around 1688-1699 and closed in 1881 due to its dilapidated condition. Hill's Charity School opened around 1808 and closed on 30 July 1965 due to a lack of pupils. These two schools were the first out of six church, five Nonconformist, three board, one Roman Catholic and one community school founded in Littleborough.

1841 saw the building of a British National, or Parish school. In June 1894, after an acrimonious campaign, the Littleborough School Board came into being. In its first year of existence, the Board, at the earnest request of the trustees because of increasing financial problems and poor reports from Her Majesty's Inspector of Schools, took over the management of four of the Nonconformist schools. The Board then undertook a campaign of building Board Schools (non-secular). Their first school, Summit Board School, opened in 1897 followed by Smithy Bridge Board School in 1900 and then finally their jewel in the crown, the Central Board School in Sale Street, opened in 1903, that school being the last to be built nationwide under the Education Act of 1870.

The last school to arrive on the scene in Littleborough was the High School, which opened in 1964 on Calderbrook Road and which now, as the Community Campus, houses a thriving community-based education and sports service. Due to falling rolls and reorganisation, only the 'primary' schools remain in Littleborough: St Andrew's, St Mary's, Holy Trinity, Stansfield, Smithy Bridge and the former Central Board School, now known as Littleborough Community Primary School and reloated in the Community Campus.

One of the classes at Hill's Endowed School, Hollingworth Fold. In 1727 a John Hill left as part of his estate the property at Hollingworth Fold and directed that £13 be provided every year from a trust to pay for a schoolmaster. When the school eventually closed, pupils were transferred to schools in Littleborough and Smithy Bridge.

The junction of Hare Hill Road with Church Street in the late 1800s, before the erection of Seed Hill Buildings, on which site stood the former hand-loom house. It was, in the late 1800s, Littleborough Technical School, but its earlier history and use is evidenced by the upper-storey windows and the taking-in door on the side. Seed Hill House can be seen, set back and to the right of the building.

The United Methodist Free Church School was the forerunner of the Central Board School and was sited on Peel Street. Whilst we cannot date the photograph accurately, we know that it was probably taken in the 1890s and before the opening of the Board School in 1903.

Above and below: The foundation stone for the Parish Church School was laid in 1877 by Mrs Beswicke of Pike House, having deposited a sealed bottle containing newspapers and other documents beneath it. The ceremony had to be hurried due to inclement weather, and a planned parade through the village was cancelled. The school was extended in 1893 by the addition of classrooms and 'closets' and, in 1909, by the addition of a single-storey section at the Lodge Street end. Mrs Beswicke's daughter, Mrs Beswicke-Royds, laid a memorial stone in July of that year. Also pictured here is the school's football team from 1937/38.

Above and below: Two photographs of teaching staff of the Central Board School, the first from 1947 and the second from 1960. Typical of the stability of education in Littleborough, both include the same headmaster and many of the same teachers. Included on the 1960 photograph are Barbara and Tom Mumford, Brenda Ratcliffe, Ruth Pearson (later to become deputy headmistress) and Brian Clegg, all of whom were still teaching at the school's successor, Littleborough High School, in the mid-1980s.

Now Stansfield Hall Church of England School, the building was originally Summit Board School and is pictured here shortly after opening in 1897. Calderbrook Terrace also looks newly built in this photograph and the top of the spire of St James' Church, Calderbrook is just visible on the right-hand side.

The Littleborough Central Board School, on Sale Street, was the last to be built in this country before the 1902 Education Act transferred powers from School Boards to the Local Authorities. In October 1894 the School Board took over the running of the Peel Street School, formerly run by the United Methodist Free Church and the Victoria Street School, formally under the management of the Littleborough Wesleyan Methodist Society from January 1879. It took eight years before support to build a purpose-designed school could be mustered, partly due to pressure exerted by the Revd Dr Salts of Holy Trinity Church who publicly declared that School Boards were ungodly and that their direct effect was to produce a nation of non-believers.

Left and below: The top photograph shows the original Sunday school on Featherstall Road opposite the junction with Whitelees Road. It was housed in an old building which eventually became too small for its needs and required much work to improve it. It was demolished and a new building erected on the site. The second photograph shows the stone-laying ceremony for the new building, which still stands today. Vulcan Terrace is the short row of cottages in the background.

Above, right and opposite page: Littleborough High School opened its doors in 1964, transferring pupils aged eleven and over primarily from the Central Board School. James Bolam was its first headmaster and these photographs were aimed at promoting the wide range of educational activities that its pupils could enjoy. Examples we see here are the school choir, vehicle maintenance club, science laboratories and gymnasium. The school taught pupils from the ages of eleven to sixteen and the original 1960s buildings were supplemented by a detached ROSLA (Raising of the School Leaving Age) fifth form block and expanded sports provision. The school closed at the end of the 1980s but continues to provide primary school education as the Central Board School, Littleborough Community Primary School, transferred there in the 1990s when the building on Sale Street was demolished. The sports centre continues to thrive and the remaining rooms are popularly used for adult education.

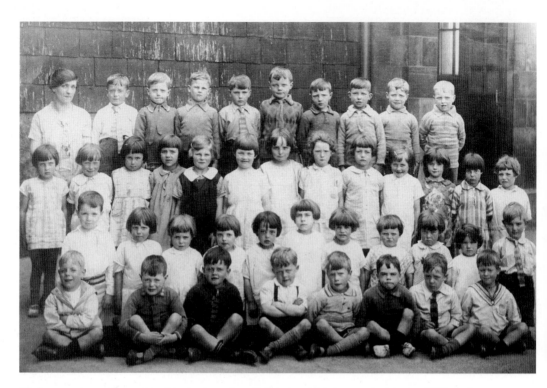

We have not been able to date this photograph so far, but we think it was taken in the 1930s. It shows one of the classes of Smithy Bridge School, complete with teacher. Any reader who is either pictured in the photograph or whose parent is pictured is welcome to contact us to confirm the age of the photograph and names of the children.

six

Landscapes

Littleborough is located in the foothills of the Pennines. The heather and gorse-covered Blackstone Edge hills (which rise to the east) and Shore Hills (which rise to the west) form the narrow wooded valley of the River Roch. It is said that before the coming of the railway, a squirrel could travel from Littleborough to Todmorden without touching the ground. The valley broadens out into the Rochdale plains and has seen many changes since the sixteenth century. Isolated houses such as Stubley Hall, Townhouse, Dearnley Hall, Windy Bank, Pike House and small hamlets such as Calderbrook, Ealees, Whittaker, Shore and Hollingworth made their appearance in the sixteenth and seventeenth centuries. Ribbon development followed the routes of the eighteenth- and nineteenth-century turnpike roads, with a recognised system of streets and terraced houses. Littleborough in the 1870s was becoming a recognisable village. Sprawling green field housing developments commenced in the 1920s.

Over forty factories and mills once dotted the landscape, together with quarries and brickworks. Whilst the open aspect of the moors is still with us, the valley bottom unfortunately is a congested built-up area where there were once wide-open spaces; nature is now covering over the scars of the industrial workings.

We are looking out of Littleborough and Lancashire into West Yorkshire to show Long Lee Chemical Works by the side of the Rochdale Canal and, on the opposite side of the valley, the buildings of Steanor Bottom Farm and the toll house itself at the junction of Todmorden Road and Calderbrook Road.

We think this aerial view of Littleborough dates from the 1920s. Several lost buildings are clearly shown, including the former Littleborough Central Board School, Littleborough Gas Works on Hare Hill Road, the Wheatsheaf Brewery and houses on the south side of Peel Street to name a few. If you look closely, you can see that buildings on the Todmorden platform of the railway station were at that time complete with a glazed canopy sheltering passengers on the platform.

Another aerial photograph, confirming Littleborough's grimy industrial past. The wharf buildings of the Brookfield Mill complex are shown in the foreground. The crane was saved when these buildings were demolished in 2004. Advertising hoardings can be seen on the Todmorden platform of the Lancashire & Yorkshire Railway line extending on to Stephenson's viaduct.

This is Stormer Bar, former toll house at the upper junction of Blackstone Edge new and old roads. The original route of the road ran past High Peak, Lydgate Mill and over Gatehouse before descending into Littleborough past Windy Bank and the Rake Inn. It ceased to be a toll house when the Local Board took over maintenance of the road in 1873.

A section of the controversial 'Roman Road' crossing Blackstone Edge. Many arguments have been proffered as to whether or not this road is of Roman origin and whilst not proven conclusively, evidence of Roman occupation of Littleborough includes the Littleborough hoard of Roman Dinarii, found at Ealees in the 1990s.

The snow-bound houses are in Lower Newgate, off Calderbrook Road and indicate the extent of the severity of winters past. Many Littleborough residents tell stories of digging tunnels through the snow to allow access to front doors. Calderbrook Road is buried under the snow.

Gorsey Hill Wood is the wooded embankment that stretches from Lower Newgate across the back of Townhouse as far as Gale. The buildings are Gorsey Hill and are at the Newgate end of the wood.

Taken from Timbercliffe, this is an excellent panorama of Calderbrook, with the Temple Methodist Chapel, Mount Gillead Chapel and St James' Parish Church clearly seen. We guess that this is a 1930s view from the location of buildings depicted.

Above and below: Two photographs of Calderbrook from Whitfield. St James' Church and Vicarage can be seen, a view not easily obtained today due to an increase in foliage following a decline in industrial pollution. The Jute Mill complex and Mill House, recently restored, are also depicted, together with houses at Higher Calderbrook which, again, are today shrouded by trees and shrubbery.

Summit Village photographed after the cessation of a tram service in the 1930s and clearly showing the Summit Brickworks and, particularly, the Hoffmann Kiln. This is a good example of the ribbon development alongside many of the main routes through the town, although in this case the narrowness of the valley floor at Summit forced such development.

An early 1900s view of Rock Nook Mill and Todmorden Road, with Calderbrook Terrace and Summit Board School. Just to the left of the Rock Nook Mill complex of Fothergill and Harvey is the chimney of Tetlow's Brickworks.

This aerial shot of Hollingworth Lake was taken in the 1960s after the demolition of Bleaked Hill Isolation Hospital. The new houses of Dale View and Knowl View are here being erected at that time. Originally built as a feeder reservoir for the Summit Level of the Rochdale Canal, the lake has been used as a pleasure ground for over 150 years, latterly becoming a country park in 1974, managed by Rochdale MBC.

Now the site of the newly extended Visitors Centre of Hollingworth Lake Country Park, the upper Ealees Valley has had several uses and its last incarnation was as municipal dump for Littleborough UDC, closed in 1974 with the reorganisation of local government.

Hollingworth Lake

Above and opposite page: Three pastoral scenes of Hollingworth Lake, a man-made reservoir created by flooding part of the valley below Hollingworth Fold to create a reserve of water used to feed the Rochdale Canal for its 150-year working life. Water was pumped from the lake to a drain set at the 600ft contour line, which fed into the canal at the Summit Level. Summit is the highest point on the Rochdale Canal and water was needed to maintain levels on both the Manchester and Calderdale sides. Within fifty years of being built, the lake was rapidly becoming a tourist trap and entrepreneurs such as James Sladen provided facilities to cater for the growing number of visitors. Excursion trains were brought to Smithy Bridge Station to swell the local population and these visitors were treated to promenades, pleasure grounds, dancing stages, boating, eating and drinking, as witnessed by these photographs. These facilities are still available today and Hollingworth Lake Country Park plays host to upwards of 1.5 million people each year who visit to participate in the wide range of recreational activities on offer.

Above and opposite page: These are three of several photographs taken during the severe winter of 1962-63 to record the snow and icy conditions experienced in Littleborough. This was the last time that the lake was substantially frozen over. The photograph opposite above is of Hollingworth Lake Rowing Club, that opposite below is Lake Bank and the photograph above looks over part of the lake towards the Sea Scouts' building on the rear bank, with boats locked into the ice.

The Hollingworth Lake Steamer. An advert in May 1856 placed in the *Rochdale Observer* by James Sladen for a pleasure steamer and paddle boats afloat on the lake everyday and Sunday evenings caused a stir in the correspondence column of the *Rochdale Observer* as it was felt that this was desecrating the Lord's Day. This steamer acted as a ferry and it cost 6d to traverse the lake.

Lake Bank, and visiting tourists experiencing the joys of boating, a pastime that is still a favourite of visitors to the lake today. The large moored boat is the *Lady Alice* and a boat bearing that name still takes visitors on circular trips round the lake.

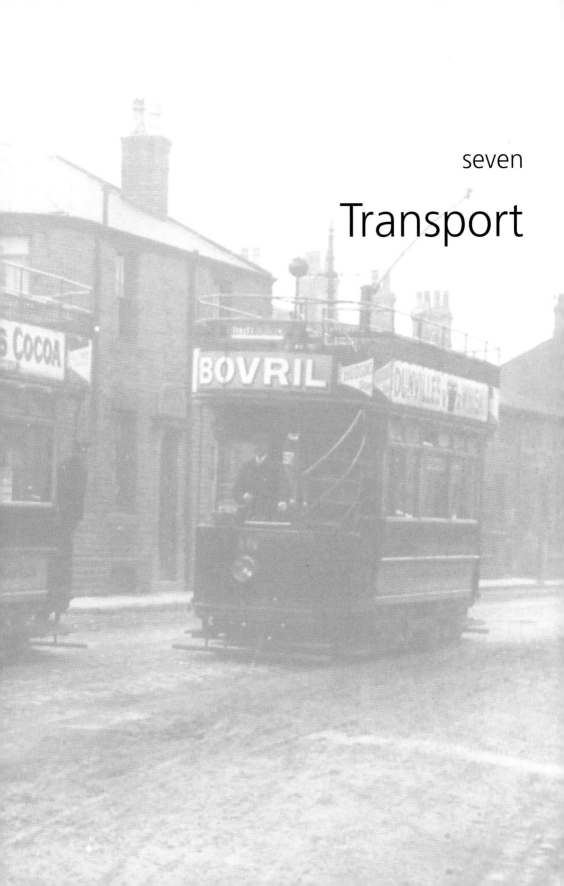

seven

Transport

Shanks' pony, horseback or, for the fortunate few, horse-drawn carriages were the chief modes of transport in Littleborough until the arrival of public transport. The complete opening of a through line of the Manchester to Leeds Railway took place on 1 March 1841. The next breakthrough came on 12 May 1877 with a horse-drawn omnibus service from the Reed Hotel in Rochdale to the Falcon Inn on Church Street. Starting in May 1889 from Cheetham Street, Rochdale, the single-line steam trams of the Manchester, Bury, Rochdale & Oldham Tramways Co. ran to the Falcon Inn in Littleborough. They were replaced on 29 May 1905 by the joint Rochdale and Littleborough electric trams running initially to Littleborough, with the line extended to Summit in August. The bicycle was a personal form of transport introduced in the late 1890s and initially owned by only a few people but later becoming a common sight, with a cycle club being formed. Trams ceased to operate in 1930 when the line was closed on 18 October that year, to be replaced on 19 October by the Rochdale Corporation Transport Department omnibus service which ran until the deregulation of public transport in the late 1980s.

All these forms of transport afforded the opportunity for the villagers to travel to work outside Littleborough and visit places of beauty and holiday resorts, so widening the horizons of Littleborough people, as well as bringing in tourists to Hollingworth Lake from other towns across the north-west of England and further afield.

A very early example of public motor vehicle transport, one of the first motorised taxis in Littleborough, in the form of Leach's Taxi. We think that this photograph was taken outside the gates of Honresfeld on Halifax Road, with the Lydgate Valley in the background.

Written on the back of this photograph is the inscription 'first car in Littleborough'. From the model and age of the vehicle – a mid-1930s Austin 7 – we think not. It's an ice cream cart conversion, the wafer cones are visible in stacks at the back, so perhaps this was the first motorised ice cream van in Littleborough. Mine's a '99', hold the raspberry!

A Maudslay three-way tipper belonging to Burrills of Springfield Avenue. Maudslay manufactured trucks in Coventry from 1903 to 1948, when they became part of AEC.

One of two vehicles, fitted with sleeper cabs, used to make multi-drop deliveries of Sun Malt loaves produced at Whittle's Bakery, seen in the background. They set off at the beginning of each week, one covered deliveries to the south of England and south coast whilst the other headed north to make deliveries in northern England and the whole of Scotland, usually returning on Thursday afternoon.

Opposite above: This is part of the early fleet of delivery vehicles of Henry Whittle's Bakery. The delivery vans are Vulcans and Model T Fords. Vulcan was based in Southport and manufactured cars from 1906 to 1927 when they went over to commercial vehicle production before becoming bankrupt in 1937. These vehicles probably date from the early 1930s.

Opposite below: A Whittle's Bakery van on the Esplanade in Rochdale outside the library, now 'Touchstones' Museum, Art Gallery and Local Studies Library, advertising both the bakery and a new loaf called the Pullman. 'Purity bread and confectionery' was Whittle's slogan.

Bent House Bridge on the Rochdale Canal sits between Durn and Rock Nook and is one of the listed structures which line the canal route. These bridges were built across the canal to allow access to farm fields dissected by the coming of the canal. Deep grooves are clearly visible in the stonework where canal boat tow ropes have worn against the side whilst horses pulled the barges along the canal. The telephone lines seen in the picture are now replaced by fibre-optic cables buried in the towpath.

Opposite: Two scenes of boats moored on the Rochdale Canal. The winter view is of Summit Level. The Summit Inn and Summit Lock House are clearly visible. It was not uncommon for the canal to freeze over in winter to the extent that boats would be locked into the ice for days or weeks at a time. A more summery aspect is depicted by the collection of boats moored at Littleborough Wharf alongside Canal Street, a good example of a typical 14ft-wide working barge that the canal was built to accommodate, rather than the more traditional 'narrowboats', the leisure craft that today ply these waters.

Above and below: The steam tram service from Rochdale terminated in Littleborough on Church Street parallel to Holy Trinity Church, where this picture was taken. The service commenced in 1882, operated by the Manchester, Bury, Rochdale & Oldham Tramways Co. and the last steam tram left Littleborough on 27 March 1905. Its replacement, the municipal electric tram, commenced service on 24 May 1905, running initially from Heybrook to Littleborough. When the service was finally extended into the centre of Rochdale, a twenty-minute journey (at a steady 14mph) cost 3d.

Eventually, the electric tram service was extended into Littleborough Square and onwards up Todmorden Road as far as Summit. This photograph was taken in the 1920s, with the catenary snaking its way up 'Gale Road' as Todmorden Road was referred to, and before demolition of the old Holy Trinity Vicarage, which can be seen nestling in a fairly small space between the road and extended church.

Trams passing each other at Featherstall. What this photograph also shows are the terraced houses which lined the St Mary's side of Whitelees Road, behind the Royal Exchange, as well as Whittle's first baker's shop on the opposite corner. The timing of trams to cross at this point extended into the omnibus service, when buses regularly passed each other at this junction.

Above and opposite: On 20 December 1984, a train pulling thirteen petrol tankers became derailed in the tunnel, spilling 40,000 gallons of fuel and causing a fire which took over three days to burn out. The Victorian tunnel withstood temperatures of 1,500°C and although the outer brick lining melted, inner linings protected the tunnel and it took only eight months for normal service to be resumed on the line, with a repair bill of £1 million.

The railway line from Littleborough to Summit was widened from two to four lines commencing in 1906, with official permission for the use of the widened lines being obtained in March 1907. Rock Nook Mill is visible in the background, where the lines once more converge to two.

Opposite above: Here are pictured the former Littleborough station signal box, up-platform buildings and the warehouse of the former Lancashire & Yorkshire Railway, which was built in 1875 and of timber construction. The signal box stands next to the existing subway, built in 1892.

Opposite below: The Smithy Bridge Rail Crash occurred on 18 March 1915 when, in bad snow visibility, a late-running Liverpool Boat Train passed through four sets of signals set at danger and ploughed into the back of a stationary stock train. The express driver and three passengers were killed, with a further thirty-one people injured.

The Rakewood Viaduct carrying the M62 from Lancashire into Yorkshire. It comprises four main spans of 150ft and two end spans of 120ft, with its highest point 140ft above the valley floor. It was opened by the Queen, making an inaugural journey on 14 October 1971.

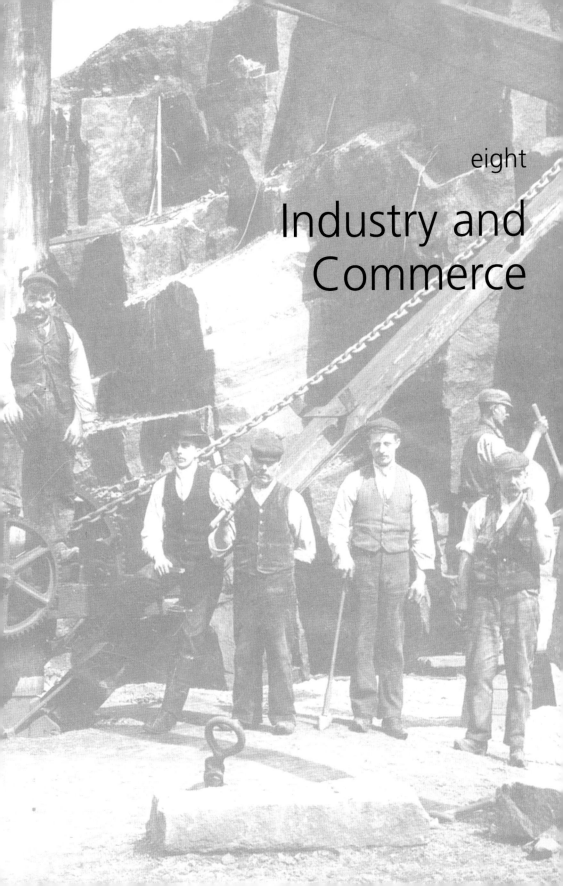

eight

Industry and Commerce

Farmhouses, loomhouses, weavers' cottages, abandoned quarries and overgrown coal slag heaps are the visible remains of industry and occupations in Littleborough from Elizabethan times to the present day. Early steam-driven mills such as Gale Mill (1820) and Townhouse Mill (1824) mirrored other northern towns in creating a factory system for the woollen and cotton industry and replaced the handloom weaver. These two industries, with their allied trades of fulling, dyeing, bleaching, finishing and calico printing dominated Littleborough's industrial scene for over 150 years. Building contractors, shuttle and picker makers, chemical, oil and grease works, bakeries, market gardens, haulage by canal and road, iron foundries, engineering works and the supply of gas, made their appearance, all becoming part of the industry of Littleborough. Eleven collieries worked the coal seams of Littleborough from the early 1800s until their closure in the 1890s. Ten brick and tile works heralded the demise of the quarry worker but fed the increased industrial and domestic building witnessed between 1846 and 1870.

In the twentieth century new industries such as leather tanning, artificial silk, asbestos, vulcanised rubber and the manufacture of plastics took the place of the declining traditional industries. These new works, like the cotton and woollen industry, made their mark on the district, but like the older industries, they too disappeared. By the end of the twentieth century many mills and works had been demolished, their sites covered by housing developments or new industrial buildings with many more diverse products forming another new generation of Littleborough industry.

Above and opposite page: Lydgate Mill, built off Blackstone Edge Old Road, was a water-powered mill, the first to be built in Littleborough by William and Alfred Law, brothers and business partners. An internal view of Lydgate Mill shows the old fulling machinery, denoting the mill's later activity. The advent of steam technology meant that mills could move off the water courses of the upper slopes into the valley floor, closer to lines of communication. Durn Mill was the result of such a move for the Law brothers. Lydgate Mill still stands, converted into luxury apartments; Durn Mill, which was built in 1866, succumbed to fire damage in May 1983 and was demolished shortly thereafter. Housing stands on the site, aptly named Durnlaw Close after the mill and its owners.

West View, Taylor Terrace leading up to Frankfort and Uber Mills on either side of Halifax Road, plus Gale Mill and the Durn branch of Littleborough Co-op, both slightly obscured in the background, together with the canal bridges of Durn, Bent House and Lightowlers. No better definition, we think, of Littleborough's industrial and commercial past.

Here's Uber Mill again, but sadly destroyed by fire on 28 September 1918 following an air raid over the Manchester and Rochdale areas during the First World War. Bystanders were killed when a wall collapsed onto an adjacent cottage. Damage was estimated to cost £27,000.

Above and below: Sladen Mill, off Blackstone Edge Road, was in the ownership of Kershaw Brothers, who described themselves as woollen manufacturers and bleachers. The Mill House stands in the background and in the foreground is the Woodcock Inn, illustrated elsewhere in this book. £125,000 worth of damage was caused by a fire at the mill on 18 January 1926. The *Rochdale Observer* described the scene that met their reporter thus: '[a] writhing mass of bent pillars, twisted iron-work and wrecked machinery ... the fire caused a vivid glare in the sky which was easily discernible in Rochdale'. The fire was assisted by the fact that Littleborough Fire Brigade were over at Ripponden dealing with a moor fire and the fire tender sent from Rochdale did not carry its own water; due to a lack of running water it was consequently of no use and was sent back to Rochdale Fire Station.

This is the old Hare Hill Mill which stood alongside the newer mill and angles into the road. Its site is now the entrance to the remaining mill complex and the higher-level car park alongside Hare Hill Road. It was demolished in the 1900s to allow for road improvements. The middle structure, standing proud of the other buildings, is the old boiler house. The mill to the right of the photograph remains standing today.

Opposite page: The first photograph shows the razing of the New Mill chimney on 24 August 1907 and obviously provided a source of much entertainment to the locals, who have surrounded the building on all sides and found vantage points wherever possible in order to watch the spectacle. The felling of the mill made way for Python Mill, home to British Visada who manufactured cellulose acetate, or artificial silk.

CHIMNEY RAZING NEW MILL LITTLEBOROUGH
AUG 24th 1909

Python Mill, Littleborough

Above and below: Two more mill disasters. This first, a fire at Gale Mill on Todmorden Road, demonstrates that mill fires were something of a spectator sport in Littleborough. The fire broke out on 22 January 1906, less than two years after a previous fire had caused extensive rebuilding of the mill by its owners, Frederick Scott & Co., calico printers. In addition to the 'throngs' pictured here, the *Rochdale Observer* reported hundreds more gathered on the hill behind the mill. The second photograph shows Clough Mill looking rather sorry for itself following a chemical explosion and fire on 1 August 1908. Whilst the *Rochdale Observer* did not report any throngs of bystanders, they did note that the sole fire-fighting efforts of employee James Hartley were 'fruitless'.

Above and below: Summit Brickworks, which was built by the Rochdale Brick & Tile Co. Ltd, was the longest surviving and technically most advanced brickworks of the several companies in the Littleborough area. The photograph shows a circular Hoffman Kiln with its central chimney. This type of kiln was invented in Germany in 1858 and the one at Summit was built in 1866 – so it was an early example. The principle products of the works were red, white and blue bricks, heating blocks and flue linings. The works was demolished shortly after it closed in 1973. The group of employees of Summit Brickworks are posing for a photograph with their backs to the Hoffman Kiln. History does not record their names. From their attire and demeanour we can determine that their work was both arduous and dirty.

Here are shown men quarrying for stone in one of several stone quarries on Blackstone Edge. The type of crane in operation and the attire of the men could date this picture as pre-First World War.

This is the loop reactor of Hess Products Ltd, the first of its kind in Europe, used in the production of fatty acids. What is now Akzo Nobel started life in 1889 as the Cleggswood Oil Distillery. It became Adolph Hess & Bros in 1925, Hess Products in 1946, Armour Hess in 1956, Akzo in 1974 and finally Akzo Nobel in 1994. The plant is now undergoing decommissioning prior to the site being sold.

The presence of tram tracks and the catenary of the Rochdale Corporation Electric Tram service date this photograph of Summit village and the post office to the 1910s or 1920s. The postmaster at Summit at the date of this photograph was an R. Parker. The cameraman appears to have caught the attention not only of the two children outside the post office but also the shopkeeper from further down the street.

From early beginnings making and selling bread and pies from Benny Hill Farm, Hollingworth Lake, Henry Whittle moved to 'The Old Post Office' pictured here at Featherstall in 1893 and by 1911 a new bakery had to be built on the land behind this building. By 1930, Henry Whittle Ltd employed over 200 people and by the 1940s that number had doubled. It was sold to Allied Bakeries (Sunblest) in 1954 and closed its doors in 1992.

The corner of Hare Hill Road and Church Street. The shops are decorated for the Silver Jubilee celebrations of King George V in 1935. Booth's shop has since been demolished, a post box marking the site.

A pre-First World War view of Hare Hill Road, with handcart, horse-drawn carriage and motor vehicle in procession. Clearly visible in the background are the Littleborough Gas Works premises, founded by the Newalls of Hare Hill House on land opposite their mill complex.

There has been a chemist shop on the corner of Hare Hill Road and Victoria Street since the buildings were erected in the 1800s. This incarnation, photographed in the late 1890s, is Athron – later it became Cravens, Geldhome and latterly Cohens.

This is a photograph of Stansfields Butchers, proudly displaying their wares outside their premises on Church Street. The two-storey cottage survives today, ivy-clad, opposite the furniture shop. Spring Vale Terrace is the row of cottages in the background. Hanging on the racks are mainly poultry and pigs and under the sign which reads 'home-fed cattle' are several silver cups, awarded to them in related competitions.

Isaac Cryer had a tobacconist shop at Lighthouse on Calderbrook Road. This is the family stood outside his premises in the late 1800s.

Joe Pilling, Iron, Copper, Zinc and Tinplate Workers, were based on Victoria Street. The building is still there today and part of a printers/IT supplies shop, a sign of the change in commercial usage for Littleborough's buildings. Their wares included milk churns, another uncommon sight in today's provision supplies.

The old coal yard on the corner of Peel Street and the station approach was in the ownership of Sorsby & Co. at the time this photograph was taken. Outside the mock-Tudor-framed office and set into the road is the old weighbridge for coal lorries and in the background, on Railway Street, is the Electric House, home to Littleborough UDC's street lighting department.

The Lancashire & Yorkshire Railway goods warehouse built adjacent to the sidings next to the railway station. It was a timber structure, erected in 1875, when the station buildings that we see today were first constructed. It was taken down when the station was reduced in size in the 1960s, together with the signal box and Rochdale platform buildings, which were also timber structures.

There had been a branch of Littleborough Co-op at Rock Nook since 1861. New premises were built and opened in 1869 and the opening was reported in the *Co-operator:* 'On Saturday Nov 4th this Society opened a branch store at Rock Nook. A tea meeting was held and a lecture delivered by Mr J.C. Farn of Eccles on the 'Causes of Co-operative Failures and Conditions of Co-operative Success'. It is now building a block of forty cottages, one half of which are already let to expectant tenants'.

Opposite above: Littleborough Co-operative Society of Industry Ltd (to give it its full title) was started in 1850 in the front room of a house on Church Street. It grew steadily over the years and by 1912 Centre Vale became the ninth premises operated by the Co-op. The building, which is located on Todmorden Road, has the initials of the Society above the main door.

Opposite below: The Co-op Boot Department. One of the many shops of the Littleborough Co-operative Society of Industry and now entrance to the Co-op Late Shop on Hare Hill Road.

Other local titles published by Tempus

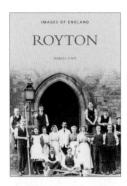

Royton
FRANCES STOTT

This collection of over 200 archive photographs traces the history of Royton as the town grew following the Industrial Revolution. Royton developed with the textile industry as mills and chimneys sprang up in the area during the Victorian era. The images will awaken nostalgic memories in people who have lived or worked in Royton, as well as providing a valuable resource for anybody interested in studying the history of the area.

0 7524 3516 7

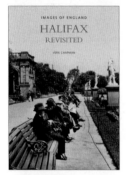

Halifax Revisited
VERA CHAPMAN

Halifax is characterised by steep slopes and deep valleys, sett-paved streets and nearby moorland. It has an industrial past of woollen mills, canals and railways, the wharves and stations of which liberally dot the countryside. The town today reflects the changes wrought by the Victorians, who created broad streets and fine buildings. This collection of over 200 archive images illustrates the history of Halifax as it once was and records how the town has developed since the mid-eighteenth century.

0 7524 3047 5

Voices of Oldham
DEREK SOUTHALL

Once the largest cotton-spinning centre in the world, Oldham was a vibrant town although many lived in poverty. The sense of community was very strong and this book records the stories and reminiscences of over thirty Oldhamers, in their own words. Their vivid voices recall childhood games, work, shops and entertainment, as well as the effects of war and bombing raids. This book is illustrated with a wealth of photographs from the personal collections of the interviewees, adding considerably to the power of their stories.

0 7524 3544 2

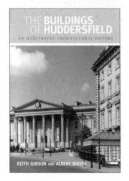

Buildings of Huddersfield
KEITH GIBSON AND ALBERT BOOTH

Huddersfield has a surprisingly rich building heritage, and this fascinating volume explores the streets of the town, documenting and discussing the buildings and architectural features which may be missed in the everyday hustle and bustle of life. Keith Gibson and Albert Booth show how the changing demands of population, business and industry have shaped the town's architecture and with a splendid series of photographs illustrates their historical narrative to great effect.

0 7524 3675 9

If you are interested in purchasing other books published by Tempus, or in case you have difficulty finding any Tempus books in your local bookshop, you can also place orders directly through our website

www.tempus-publishing.com